NINE EASY WAYS TO APPROACH MENTAL HEALTH CHALLENGES

Published by Spines
ISBN: 979-8-89691-300-9

NINE EASY WAYS TO APPROACH MENTAL HEALTH CHALLENGES

THE ONE SHOP MENTAL HEALTH OUTLET

SHAKIR MARIS ABDULLAH

CONTENTS

DEDICATION

Praise belongs to God, the Cherisher, Sustainer, and Protector of mankind, who guides to ways and paths to approach and solve human problems.

A person (man or woman), actual personal life depends upon many things:

1. Their personal psychology,
2. The background of their life,
3. Their tendencies,
4. Their antipathies,
5. Their hereditary disposition,
6. History,
7. Their education,
8. Their environment,
9. Their hidden or repressed feelings.

All of the above life experiences should be viewed or studied collectively or simultaneously when looking at ones own life! This cluster life-experience approach would give individuals an in-depth view of their own life and possibly point to life experiences that need to be addressed forthwith for a balanced well-being.

Welcome to the one-shop mental health outlet, where shopping for mental health solutions has never been so easy.

INTRODUCTION

This document outlines the plan for the "One Shop Mental Health Outlet" expansion, focusing on mental health and well-being. It is divided into several key sections:

Chapter 1: Psychology

- Understanding the science of the mind, various branches of psychology, and practical ways to apply psychological principles for better mental health.

Chapter 2: Background of Life

- Examining how early life experiences, adolescence, adulthood, and aging contribute to mental health.
  - Includes reflection exercises and six case

studies to highlight the importance of personal history.

Chapter 3: Tendencies

- Analyzing habitual behaviors that influence mental well-being, from procrastination to overthinking.
  - Steps to identify, modify, and transform these tendencies for growth.

Chapter 4: Antipathies

- Understanding aversions or dislikes and their impact on emotional balance.
  - Strategies to challenge biases, confront fears, and cultivate acceptance.

Chapter 5: Hereditary Disposition

- Exploring the role of genetics in mental health, understanding the interplay of nature and nurture, and practical steps to mitigate hereditary risks while fostering resilience.

Chapter 6: History

- The influence of personal and societal history on

mental well-being, including the long-term impact of collective experiences.

Chapter 7: Education

- The transformative power of learning in building emotional intelligence, resilience, and self-awareness.
  - Real-life examples of how education contributes to mental health.

Chapter 8: Environment

- Exploring the influence of physical and social surroundings on emotional health.
  - Steps to create supportive environments for personal and communal well-being.

Chapter 9: Hidden or Repressed Feelings

- Uncovering and processing emotions buried in the subconscious.
  - Tools such as journaling, mindfulness, and therapeutic support are discussed, along with real-life examples and exercises.

These chapters aim to provide readers with a holistic

approach to mental health and practical solutions for improving well-being.

PSYCHOLOGY

Introduction to Psychology

Psychology is the scientific study of the mind and behavior. It explores various processes, including perception, cognition, emotion, personality, and social interactions. Understanding psychology is the first step toward improving mental health as it provides insights into how we think, feel, and behave.

Importance of Psychology in Mental Health

Psychology plays a critical role in mental well-being by helping individuals understand their emotions, thoughts, and behaviors. Through therapeutic techniques and interventions, psychology aims to enhance overall well-being and reduce mental distress.

Key Psychological Concepts

1. **Cognition**: Refers to mental processes such as thinking, reasoning, and problem-solving.
2. **Emotion**: Involves feelings such as happiness, sadness, anger, and fear, which significantly influence our mental state.
3. **Behavior**: Refers to actions or reactions of individuals in response to external or internal stimuli.
4. **Personality**: Represents the unique and enduring patterns of thoughts, feelings, and behaviors that characterize an individual.

Psychological Approaches

1. **Behavioral Psychology**: Focuses on observable behaviors and how they are learned through conditioning.
2. **Cognitive Psychology**: Studies mental processes like memory, perception, and problem-solving.
3. **Humanistic Psychology**: Emphasizes personal growth and self-fulfillment.
4. **Psychodynamic Psychology**: Explores unconscious motivations and early childhood experiences.
5. **Biopsychosocial Model**: Considers biological,

psychological, and social factors in understanding health and illness.

Practical Applications of Psychology

1. **Therapy and Counseling**: Techniques to help individuals manage and overcome mental health issues.
2. **Mindfulness and Meditation**: Practices to enhance awareness and reduce stress.
3. **Behavior Modification**: Strategies to change unhealthy habits and promote positive behaviors.
4. **Cognitive Behavioral Therapy (CBT)**: Combines cognitive and behavioral techniques to address dysfunctional thinking patterns.
5. **Detailed Overview of Psychology**: Includes definitions, subfields (e.g., clinical, developmental, cognitive), and their contributions to mental health.
6. **Real-Life Example**: A young adult struggling with anxiety uses cognitive-behavioral techniques to challenge negative thoughts.
7. **Case Study**: Maria, a 32-year-old teacher, benefits from psychodynamic therapy to address childhood trauma.
8. **Applications of Psychology**: Explores modern therapy models like CBT, mindfulness, and

positive psychology, which promote resilience and well-being.

Understanding the Science of the Mind

Psychology is the cornerstone of understanding mental health. It examines how people think, feel, and behave, offering insights into what drives human actions. By understanding psychology, individuals can take control of their mental well-being and make informed decisions about their lives.

What is Psychology?

Psychology is both a science and an art. It involves studying mental processes and behaviors scientifically and applying that knowledge to improve understanding and manage emotions, relationships, and interpersonal dynamics. Psychology provides a comprehensive framework for self-awareness and growth.

Branches of Psychology

1. **Clinical Psychology**: Focuses on diagnosing and treating mental disorders.
2. **Developmental Psychology**: Explores how people grow and change over a lifetime.
3. **Cognitive Psychology**: Examines mental processes such as memory, decision-making, problem-solving, and reasoning.

4. **Social Psychology**: Investigates how social interactions influence behavior and emotions.

Why Psychology is Vital for Mental Health

Understanding psychological principles allows individuals to:

- Identify triggers for stress, anxiety, or depression.
- Develop coping mechanisms.
- Strengthen relationships by understanding others' perspectives.
- Build resilience in the face of challenges.

Practical Applications of Psychology

Psychological knowledge isn't limited to therapy rooms; it impacts various aspects of life:

1. **In Education**: Teachers use psychology to manage classrooms and support diverse learners.
2. **In Workplaces**: Employers apply psychological principles to boost employee motivation and satisfaction.
3. **In Everyday Life**: People practice mindfulness to reduce stress and enhance focus.

Real-Life Example: Anxiety Management

Sarah, a college student, struggled with anxiety during

exams. She experienced sweating, difficulty concentrating, and intrusive thoughts. Through cognitive-behavioral therapy (CBT), Sarah learned to challenge irrational fears and replace them with positive affirmations. With practice, she regained confidence and improved her academic performance.

Common Misconceptions About Psychology

1. **"Psychology is just common sense."**
   - Fact: Psychology relies on scientific research and evidence-based practices.
2. **"Therapy is only for people with severe issues."**
   - Fact: Anyone can benefit from therapy, whether managing daily stress or seeking personal growth.

Case Study: Overcoming Emotional Burnout

- **Background**: Tom, a 40-year-old software engineer, experienced emotional burnout due to long working hours and high-pressure deadlines. He felt irritable, disconnected, and unmotivated.
- **Intervention**: Tom sought help from a psychologist who introduced him to mindfulness-based stress reduction (MBSR). By practicing daily meditation and focusing on small, achievable goals, Tom gradually regained his sense of balance.
- **Outcome**: After eight weeks, Tom reported

reduced stress levels, improved focus, and better relationships with colleagues and family.

Steps to Apply Psychological Insights

1. **Reflect on Your Behavior**: Keep a journal to track thoughts and emotions.
2. **Learn Stress Management Techniques**: Practice mindfulness or deep-breathing exercises.
3. **Seek Professional Guidance**: Consult a psychologist when struggling with persistent issues.
4. **Build Emotional Awareness**: Identify patterns in your reactions to different situations.

Psychology helps individuals understand themselves and others better. By applying its principles, anyone can enhance their mental health and lead a more fulfilling life.

BACKGROUND OF LIFE

The Role of Life Experiences

Our life experiences shape who we are and how we view the world. These experiences profoundly impact our mental health, influencing our thoughts, emotions, and behaviors.

Early Childhood

Early childhood is a crucial period for mental health development. The environment in which a child grows up, including the care they receive and the relationships they form, significantly affects their psychological well-being.

Adolescence

Adolescence is a period when individuals begin to form their identity and navigate complex social dynamics.

Support and guidance are essential during these formative years for maintaining mental health.

Adulthood

Adulthood presents its own set of challenges, including career pressures, relationship dynamics, and life transitions. Understanding and managing these challenges are vital for maintaining mental well-being.

Aging and Mental Health

Aging brings changes in both physical and mental health. It is important to address the unique mental health needs of older adults, including coping with loss, maintaining social connections, and managing chronic health conditions.

Coping with Life's Challenges

1. **Problem-Solving Skills**: Techniques to effectively address and resolve issues.
2. **Stress Management**: Practices like relaxation techniques and time management to reduce stress.
3. **Emotional Regulation**: Strategies to manage and express emotions in healthy ways.
4. **Support Systems**: Building strong relationships and seeking support from friends, family, and professionals.

Foundation of Mental Health

Life Experiences Shape Us

Life experiences mold our perception of ourselves and the world around us. From early childhood to old age, these experiences influence our mental health and emotional resilience. Understanding our background allows us to connect the dots between our past, present, and future, paving the way for healing and growth.

1. The Early Years

Childhood is a critical period for mental health development. Experiences during this time form the basis for emotional security, self-esteem, and interpersonal relationships.

Parental Influence: A nurturing environment fosters confidence, while neglect or inconsistency can lead to anxiety and attachment issues.

- **Example:** A child raised in a supportive household may develop a positive self-image, while one exposed to constant criticism might struggle with self-doubt.

2. Adolescence and Mental Health

Adolescence is a time of self-discovery and rapid change. The transition from childhood to adulthood brings challenges such as peer pressure, academic expectations, and identity exploration.

Emotional Regulation: Teens often experience mood swings due to hormonal changes and evolving cognitive abilities.

- **Example:** Emma, a high school student, felt overwhelmed by the need to fit in. Through journaling and counseling, she learned to embrace her personal values.

3. Adulthood: Balancing Responsibilities

Adulthood introduces a mix of opportunities and pressures, from career advancement to building relationships.

Work-Life Balance: Struggling to manage time between professional and personal commitments can lead to stress.

Life Transitions: Events like marriage, parenthood, or relocating often bring joy and stress in equal measure.

- **Example:** James, a new father, experienced anxiety about providing for his family.

4. Aging and Reflection

As people age, they reflect on their life and accomplishments. Some experience fulfillment, while others grapple with regret or loneliness.

Physical and Mental Health: Chronic illnesses or mobility challenges can impact mental health.

- **Example:** Linda, a 70-year-old widow, found solace in community volunteering, which improved her mood and gave her a sense of purpose.

5. Case Study: Overcoming Childhood Trauma

Background: Michael, a 28-year-old graphic designer, struggled with low self-esteem and difficulty trusting others. Growing up in a home with frequent arguments and emotional neglect, he often felt isolated.

Intervention: Through therapy, Michael worked to identify how his childhood experiences shaped his current behaviors. His therapist introduced techniques like inner-child work and affirmations to rebuild his self-worth.

Outcome: Michael improved his relationships, set healthy boundaries, and reconnected with his passions, finding fulfillment and confidence.

6. Life's Challenges and Coping Mechanisms

- **Identify Patterns:** Reflect on recurring themes in your life—successes, setbacks, and turning points.
- **Develop Emotional Awareness:** Recognize how past experiences influence current emotions.

- **Practice Resilience:** Embrace challenges as opportunities for growth.

7. Practical Exercise: Mapping Your Life Journey

Step 1: Draw a timeline of your life, marking key events (both positive and negative).

Step 2: Reflect on how each event shaped your mental health.

Step 3: Identify lessons learned and areas needing healing.

- **Example:** A reader maps their journey, recognizing that a high school mentor sparked their love for writing, while a failed relationship taught them the importance of self-care.

Moving Forward

The background of your life isn't just about what has happened—it's about what you make of it. This chapter provides a roadmap for readers to reflect on their past, draw meaningful insights, and begin their journey toward mental health.

UNDERSTANDING TENDENCIES

Tendencies are habitual patterns of behavior, thought, or emotion that can influence our mental health. Recognizing and understanding our tendencies is the first step toward making positive changes.

Common Psychological Tendencies

- **Perfectionism:** Striving for flawlessness and setting high standards.
- **Procrastination:** Delaying tasks and decisions.
- **Pessimism:** Focusing on negative aspects of situations.
- **Optimism:** Focusing on positive aspects of situations.
- **Anxiety:** Experiencing excessive worry or fear.

Identifying Personal Tendencies

Self-awareness is crucial for identifying personal tendencies. Reflecting on past behaviors and emotional responses can help individuals understand their habitual patterns.

Modifying Unhealthy Tendencies

Overcoming unhealthy tendencies involves these steps:

1. **Awareness:** Recognizing the tendency and its impact on mental health.
2. **Understanding:** Exploring the underlying causes.
3. **Strategies:** Developing and implementing strategies to modify the tendency.
4. **Support:** Seeking guidance from mental health professionals or support groups.

Cultivating Positive Tendencies

- **Mindfulness:** Practicing mindfulness to increase awareness and reduce automatic reactions.
- **Gratitude:** Fostering gratitude to enhance overall well-being.
- **Resilience:** Building resilience to better cope with stress and adversity.
- **Empathy:** Developing empathy to improve social connections and emotional intelligence.
- **Types of Tendencies:** Explaining behaviors in-depth.

- **Practical Examples:** For instance, how procrastination impacts a college student's grades and mental health.
- **Case Study:** Sarah, a perfectionist, learns to set realistic goals through counseling.
- **Behavioral Change:** Steps to identify and modify unhelpful tendencies with real-world applications.

Common Tendencies

1. Procrastination: Delaying important tasks, often due to fear of failure or lack of motivation.

Example: A student postpones studying until the night before an exam, resulting in poor performance and heightened anxiety.

2. Overthinking: Excessively analyzing situations, leading to mental exhaustion.

Example: A woman repeatedly replays a past conversation, doubting her words and intentions.

3. Impulsivity: Acting without considering consequences.

Example: A man spends beyond his budget during a shopping spree, causing financial stress.

Case Study: Transforming a Negative Tendency

Background:

Anna, a marketing professional, struggled with chronic

procrastination. Deadlines became a source of panic, and her work quality suffered.

Intervention:

A productivity coach introduced Anna to time-blocking techniques and the Pomodoro method. Therapy helped her address underlying fears of judgment.

Outcome:

Over three months, Anna's productivity improved significantly. She met deadlines with ease and gained confidence in her abilities.

Practical Steps to Modify Tendencies

1. **Identify Triggers:** Recognize situations that lead to negative tendencies.
2. **Replace Patterns:** Develop constructive habits to counteract them.
3. **Set Small Goals:** Break tasks into manageable steps to build consistency.

ANTIPATHIES

DEFINING ANTIPATHIES:

Antipathies refer to strong feelings of dislike or aversion toward certain people, situations, or things. These negative feelings can impact mental health and relationships.

Sources of Antipathies:

Antipathies can stem from past experiences, cultural influences, or personal values. Understanding their origins is essential for managing and overcoming them.

Impact on Mental Health:

Left unaddressed, antipathies can affect overall well-being, making it vital to tackle them for a healthier mindset.

Managing and Overcoming Antipathies:

- **Self-Reflection:** Identify the root causes and reflect on their impact.

- **Empathy:** Develop understanding toward others.
- **Communication:** Engage in open, respectful discussions to resolve conflicts.
- **Acceptance:** Practice letting go of negative feelings.

Cultivating Positive Attitudes:

- **Forgiveness:** Release grudges and embrace forgiveness.
- **Open-Mindedness:** Welcome new perspectives and adapt to change.
- **Positive Thinking:** Focus on constructive aspects and use affirmations.

Understanding Antipathies

Types of Antipathies:

1. **Social Antipathies:** Discomfort in specific social settings.
2. **Situational Antipathies:** Aversions triggered by environments or tasks.
3. **Cultural Antipathies:** Prejudices shaped by societal norms or biases.

Example:

A manager learns to overcome unconscious bias, enabling the building of a diverse team.

Case Study:

Tom, who dislikes crowds due to childhood experiences, discovers the root of his aversion and gradually overcomes it through therapy and exposure exercises.

Steps to Address Antipathies:

1. **Acknowledge Biases:** Recognize the origins of your aversions.
2. **Gradual Exposure:** Confront aversions incrementally to build tolerance.

HEREDITARY DISPOSITION

ROLE OF GENETICS IN MENTAL HEALTH:

Genetics significantly influence predispositions to certain mental health conditions. Understanding hereditary factors provides insights into potential risks.

Genetic Factors and Mental Health Conditions:

Some conditions, such as depression, anxiety, and schizophrenia, have a genetic component. Awareness of family history is key to early intervention.

Managing Hereditary Risks:

1. **Awareness:** Understand family history and potential risks.
2. **Prevention:** Adopt healthy lifestyle choices and undergo regular check-ups.
3. **Support:** Seek guidance from mental health professionals.

4. **Education:** Learn about conditions and effective management strategies.

The Role of Epigenetics:

Epigenetics explores how environmental factors influence gene expression. Lifestyle choices and surroundings can significantly affect mental health outcomes.

Strategies for Enhancing Mental Health:

1. **Healthy Lifestyle:** Maintain a balanced diet and exercise regularly.
2. **Stress Management:** Practice mindfulness and relaxation techniques.
3. **Social Support:** Build strong connections with others.
4. **Professional Help:** Seek assistance from qualified professionals and follow prescribed treatments.
5. **Example:** A family with a history of bipolar disorder learns prevention strategies.
6. **Case Study:** Emily, aware of her genetic predisposition for schizophrenia, adopts a proactive lifestyle to mitigate risks.

Role of Genetics in Mental Health

Understanding Hereditary Disposition

Mental health conditions like depression, anxiety, and bipolar disorder often have a genetic component. While genes influence disposition, environmental factors and lifestyle choices also play crucial roles.

- **Example: Family Patterns**
- Families with a history of anxiety disorders often display similar symptoms across generations. Early intervention can mitigate risks.
- **Case Study: Managing Genetic Risk**
  - **Background:** Lisa, whose mother and grandmother battled depression, feared inheriting the condition.
  - **Intervention:** Through proactive strategies, including therapy and mindfulness, she addressed her concerns.
  - **Outcome:** Despite her genetic predisposition, Lisa maintained a positive outlook and managed stress effectively.

Strategies for Balancing Nature and Nurture

1. **Understand Your Family History:** Identify patterns of mental health issues.

2. **Adopt a Healthy Lifestyle:** Prioritize habits that support mental wellness.

3. **Seek Preventive Care:** Consult professionals for early guidance.

HISTORY

Influence of Personal History on Mental Health

Personal history, including past experiences and significant life events, shapes mental health. Understanding one's history provides valuable insights into current mental health issues and guides therapeutic interventions.

- **Childhood Experiences:**
- Childhood trauma, neglect, or abuse can have lasting impacts on mental health. Early intervention is crucial to addressing these issues.
- **Traumatic Events:**
- Events like accidents, loss, or violence can lead to conditions such as PTSD. Addressing trauma is essential for recovery.
- **Life Transitions:**
- Significant changes, such as moving, career shifts,

or personal losses, can affect mental health. Coping strategies help navigate these transitions.

Healing from the Past

1. **Acknowledgment:** Recognize and understand the impact of past experiences.
2. **Support:** Build a network of friends, family, and professionals.
3. **Self-Compassion:** Practice self-care to foster healing.

Moving Forward

- **Letting Go:** Release past hurts and focus on the present.
- **Growth:** Embrace personal development and resilience.
- **Positive Outlook:** Cultivate optimism and set future goals.
- **Expanded Content:**
  - **Trauma Example:** A veteran overcoming PTSD through therapy.
  - **Case Study:** A woman overcoming an abusive childhood with EMDR therapy.

EDUCATION

Role of Education in Mental Health

Education significantly impacts mental health by fostering knowledge, skills, and opportunities for growth. It influences cognitive development and emotional well-being.

- **Early Childhood Education:**
- Positive early education experiences promote resilience and mental health.
- **Academic Achievement:**
- Academic success affects self-esteem and confidence. Supportive environments enhance mental well-being.
- **Lifelong Learning:**
- Keeping the mind engaged supports mental health, offering opportunities for growth and skill development.

Education and Mental Health Awareness

Education helps reduce stigma around mental health issues. Schools, workplaces, and communities play vital roles in promoting mental health education and resources.

Strategies for Promoting Mental Health Through Education

1. **Supportive Environments:** Create inclusive and safe learning spaces.
2. **Mental Health Resources:** Provide access to mental health support.
3. **Skill Development:** Teach emotional regulation, problem-solving, and stress management.
4. **Social-Emotional Learning:** Schools integrating SEL programs report reduced bullying.
5. **Case Study:** A dropout rebuilds self-esteem through adult education programs.

ENVIRONMENT

Impact of Environment on Mental Health

The physical surroundings and social contexts of an individual significantly influence mental health. A positive environment fosters well-being, while adverse conditions can exacerbate challenges.

The Influence of Surroundings on Mental Health

Physical Environment

The physical environment, including housing, neighborhoods, and access to green spaces, can significantly influence mental health. Clean, safe, and supportive surroundings promote well-being.

- **Example**: Urban residents benefit from community gardens and public parks, which provide opportunities for relaxation and connection with nature.

Social Environment

The social environment, encompassing relationships, community, and cultural influences, plays a crucial role in mental health. Positive social connections and a sense of belonging are essential for emotional well-being.

- **Case Study**: After moving to a new city, Jane felt isolated and anxious. Joining a local book club provided her with meaningful connections, significantly improving her mental health.

Workplace Environment

The workplace environment impacts mental health through factors like workload, relationships with colleagues, and organizational culture. Supportive workplace policies and practices enhance well-being.

- **Example**: A factory worker thrived after their company introduced ergonomic workstations and counseling services.

Strategies for Creating a Positive Environment

1. **Home**: Create a safe, comfortable, and nurturing space by decluttering and organizing.
2. **Communities**: Foster supportive communities and build meaningful social connections.
3. **Workplace**: Promote mental health-friendly workplace policies and practices.
4. **Nature**: Spend time in green spaces to reduce stress and enhance overall well-being.

HIDDEN OR REPRESSED FEELINGS

What Are Hidden or Repressed Feelings?

Hidden or repressed feelings are emotions buried deep within the subconscious, often to avoid pain or discomfort. These emotions remain unaddressed, subtly influencing thoughts and behaviors.

- **Examples**:
    - Anger disguised as sarcasm.
    - Sadness masked by constant busyness.
    - Fear hidden under excessive control.

Causes of Repressed Feelings

1. **Cultural and Societal Expectations**: Societies discouraging emotional expression often lead individuals to suppress their feelings.

- ○ **Example**: A boy taught to "be tough" may grow up avoiding vulnerability, leading to emotional disconnection.

2. **Trauma**: Painful experiences can result in emotional suppression as a coping mechanism.
3. **Family Dynamics**: Families that discourage open communication foster emotional repression.

Signs of Repressed Feelings

- **Physical Symptoms**: Chronic tension, headaches, or fatigue.
- **Behavioral Patterns**: Avoidance, overreaction, or numbing behaviors like overeating or excessive screen time.
- **Emotional Outbursts**: Bottled-up emotions may surface as sudden anger or sadness.

Why Address Repressed Feelings?

Unaddressed emotions can manifest as mental health challenges like anxiety, depression, or low self-esteem. Processing these feelings promotes:

- Reduced stress and improved well-being.
- Stronger relationships through emotional authenticity.
- Personal growth and self-awareness.

Practical Examples of Uncovering Repressed Feelings

1. **Confronting Guilt**: Jane, a nurse, repaired her relationship with a friend after addressing guilt from a past fallout.
2. **Rediscovering Joy**: Mark, a retired athlete, connected with his purpose by exploring grief over his career's end and began mentoring young athletes.
3. **Overcoming Anger**: Alex, a software developer, identified resentment toward his parents through journaling and therapy. Assertive communication improved his relationships and emotional balance.

Tools for Processing Hidden Emotions

1. **Journaling**: Write down thoughts and feelings to bring emotions to light.
2. **Mindfulness Practices**: Techniques like meditation increase emotional awareness and acceptance.
3. **Therapeutic Support**: Seek therapies like psychodynamic counseling or somatic experiencing to process emotions.
4. **Artistic Expression**: Use painting, music, or writing as outlets for emotional expression.

Exercises to Unlock Repressed Feelings

1. **Emotion Reflection**: Write down emotions you frequently feel and those you rarely acknowledge. Reflect on why certain emotions are avoided.
2. **"Empty Chair" Technique**: Imagine speaking to someone tied to unresolved emotions and express your thoughts aloud.
3. **Body Scan Meditation**: Focus on areas of tension in your body and associate them with suppressed emotions.

Moving Forward

Processing hidden or repressed feelings is a journey requiring patience, self-compassion, and commitment to emotional authenticity. By addressing these buried emotions, individuals unlock a sense of freedom, authenticity, and mental well-being.

CONCLUSION

This comprehensive guide provides insightful approaches to mental health and emotional growth. Through in-depth explanations, practical examples, and case studies, it encourages the development of a new mental health movement that prioritizes well-being and authenticity.